LOXI

THE LOP EARED BUNNY

by Jenny Schreiber

Loxi the Lop Eared Bunny
Adventures of the Mini Lop Eared Rabbit (Pre Reader)

©2023 Jenny Schreiber

In Association with:
Elite Online Publishing
63 East 11400 South
Suite #230
Sandy, UT 84070
EliteOnlinePublishing.com

ISBN: 978-1-961801-14-1 (Paperback)
ISBN: 978-1-961801-15-8 (Hardback)

LOXI

THE LOP EARED BUNNY

by Jenny Schreiber

Meet Loxi the mini lop eared bunny.

Loxi the mini lop rabbit is a great pet for a family.

She has long ears
that flop down,
which is why she is
called a "mini lop."

Loxi is a brown bunny, but her brothers and sisters come in many different colors, like white, brown, black, and gray.

Loxi loves to hop around and play, especially in large and spacious areas.

Loxi needs a cozy place to sleep, called a hutch or cage, with soft bedding.

She eats yummy
foods like hay,
fresh vegetables,
and special bunny
pellets.

Loxi likes to munch on carrots, which is her favorite treat.

Mini lop bunnies
have teeth that
grow continuously,
so they need to
chew on things to
keep them trimmed.

Loxi loves to have her silky fur softly stroked, especially behind her ears.

She has a cute nose that wiggles when she is curious or sniffing around.

Loxi is a social animal and likes to have bunny friends to play with.

Loxi can learn tricks,
like jumping
through hoops or
coming when called.

Loxi needs plenty of exercise, so she should have time to hop and explore outside her cage.

Loxi is a very clean animal and grooms herself by licking her fur.

She has strong
hind legs that help
her jump high
and run fast.

Mini lop bunnies communicate with each other by making soft sounds or thumping their back feet.

Loxi has big, expressive eyes that can see very well, especially in the dark.

Loxi loves to dig in the dirt and create little burrows or tunnels.

Loxi enjoys playing with toys, like balls or tunnels, to keep her entertained.

Mini lop bunnies make wonderful pets and companions. They can bring lots of joy and happiness to a family.

Find More books by Jenny Schreiber

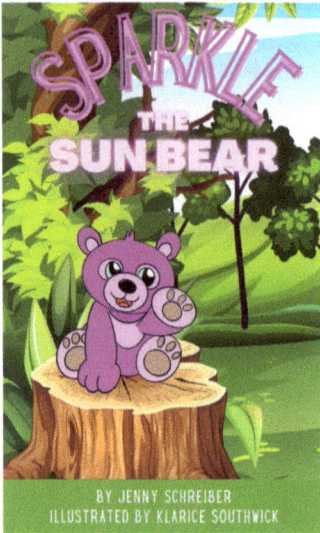

Sparkle the Sun Bear

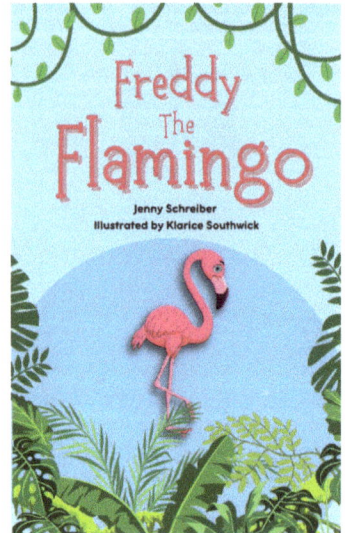

Freddy the Flamingo

Piper the
Polar Bear

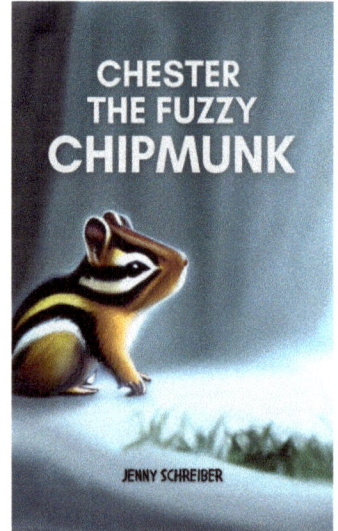

Chester the
Fuzzy Chipmunk

Animal Facts Children's Book Series

Paige the
Panda Bear

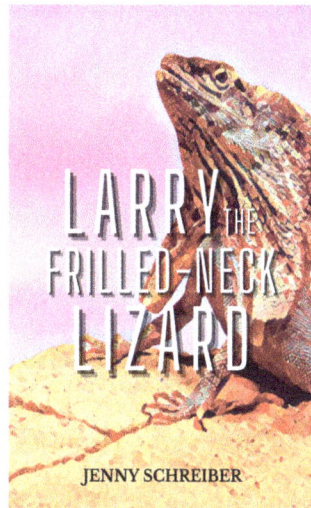

Larry the
Frilled-Neck Lizard

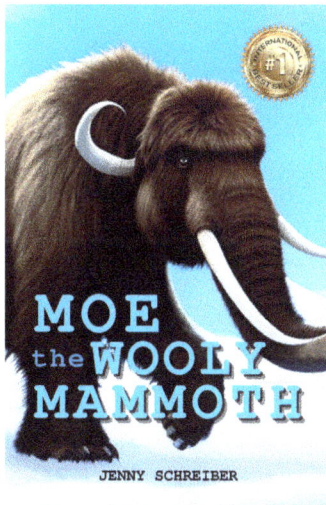

Moe the
Wooly Mammoth

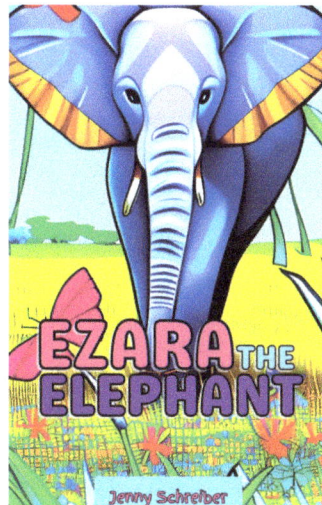

Ezara the
Elephant

www.ingramcontent.com/pod-product-compliance
Lightning Source LLC
Chambersburg PA
CBHW052123030426
42335CB00025B/3093